BEFORE YOU WERE BORN

BEFORE YOU WERE BORN

Written by Margaret Sheffield

Illustrated by Sheila Bewley

Alfred A. Knopf
New York   1984

THIS IS A BORZOI BOOK
PUBLISHED BY ALFRED A. KNOPF, INC.

———————————————————————————

Copyright © 1983 by Margaret Sheffield and Sheila Bewley

All rights reserved under International and Pan-American
Copyright Conventions. Published in the United States by
Alfred A. Knopf, Inc., New York. Originally published in
Great Britain by Jonathan Cape Ltd., London. Distributed
by Random House, Inc., New York.

Library of Congress Cataloging in Publication Data

Sheffield, Margaret.
    Before you were born.

    Summary: Describes what life is like for a baby growing
inside its mother's womb during the months before birth, and
what it is like to be born.
    1. Pregnancy—Juvenile literature. [1. Pregnancy.
2. Childbirth. 3. Babies] I. Bewley, Sheila, ill. II. Title.
RG525.5.S53   1984   612'.63   83-48930
ISBN 0-394-53734-3

Manufactured in the United States of America

FIRST AMERICAN EDITION

BEFORE YOU WERE BORN

7056584

Your body is young and strong. It is cuddly and warm. It is different from anybody else's body, although it is made to the same pattern. Do you suck your thumb like the child in the picture?

When you were a little baby you used to get your food by sucking.

Before you were born you were inside your mother in a special place called the womb, and lots of the things you do now you started to do then—even sucking.

When you go to sleep, do you curl up like a ball?

When you were inside your Mommy you spent a lot of time curled up like that, asleep. You were safe in there. You were joined to your Mommy with a cord.

At first, boys and girls look the same. But by the time a baby has been growing for only two months, you could tell, if you could look inside, whether it was going to be a boy or a girl.

This is a girl.

This is a boy.

Can you swim underwater? It used to be easy. During
your life before you were born you were floating in
warm, salty water, rather like seawater. You didn't have
to worry about breathing, because you didn't breathe
air then. Your Mommy breathed for you.

You didn't have to worry about eating either. You shared your Mommy's food. What you needed from the air she breathed and the food she ate came to you through the cord which joined you together. The end of the cord used to be where your belly-button is now.

But you had your own heart, and people could even hear it beating from the outside.

You didn't spend all your time sleeping. You could kick your legs and arms. You could even stand on your head.

Your Mommy could feel where your head was, because it made a big bulge in her tummy. Your head was the biggest part of you. What were you thinking about?

Although you often had your eyes open, you couldn't see, because it is dark in the womb. But you could hear. You could hear your Mommy's body creaking and rumbling like an old house at night.

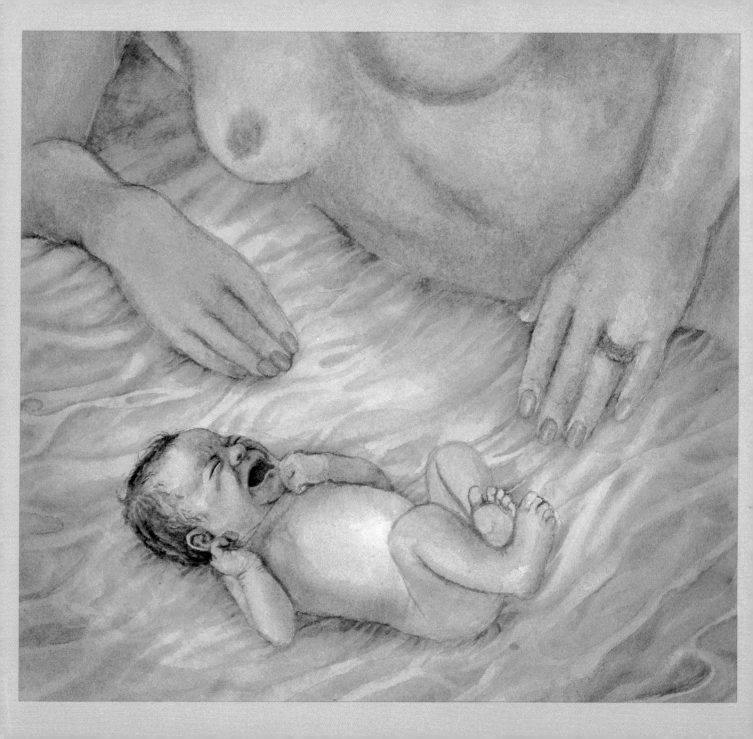

Being born was quite an adventure. Most babies are born headfirst. They come down the vagina and out between their mothers' legs.

When you were inside you couldn't talk or cry. But you gave a big yell the moment you got out.

Outside it was bright and noisy. You felt the cold air on your skin, and breathed it in for the first time. You opened your eyes and you could see. You saw your Mommy for the first time, face to face, and she saw you.

ABOUT THE AUTHORS

Margaret Sheffield, who was born in New Zealand and took a Science degree at the University of Otago, taught in New Zealand and London before joining the B.B.C., where she is currently a writer and producer of radio and television programmes.

Sheila Bewley, who studied illustration at St. Martin's School of Art, now lives in Cornwall and works as an illustrator, printmaker and teacher.

A NOTE ON THE TYPE

This book was set in a film version of De Vinne, an American type face that was a recutting by Gustav Schroeder of French Elzevir. It was introduced by the Central Type Foundry of St. Louis in 1889. Named in honor of Theodore Low De Vinne, whose nine-story plant called ''The Fortress'' was the first building in New York City erected expressly for printing, the type has a delicate quality obtained by the contrast between the thick and thin parts of letters. An enormously popular type during the early part of this century, De Vinne combines easy readability with a nostalgically atmospheric feeling.

Typography and binding design by Virginia Tan